MY GARDEN VISITS

Written by Justin Matott
Illustrated by Victoria Kwasinski

CLOVE PUBLICATIONS
Littleton, Colorado

Published by
CLOVE PUBLICATIONS
PO Box 261183
Littleton, Colorado 80163-1183

ISBN 1-889191-08-6

Book layout and design by
Victoria Kwasinski

Printed in the United States of America

MY GARDEN VISITS

◆ FOR ◆

Julia Matott,
who found solace in the cultivation
of life's experiences.
We miss you.

Glenn Matott,
for hours of encouragement and editing.

My beloved wife, Andy,
for belief, patience, and love.

Ron Harris Jr.,
for inspiring me to write.
- J.M.

Joe and Mollie, Mom and Dad,
Family and Friends,
for love, support, and encouragement.

Dianne Murtaugh,
for showing me how to
"listen to my heart"
and "follow my dreams".
- V.K.

CONTENTS

INTRODUCTION

Oddly enough, it is the ordinary weed that has brought me balance and a more healthy outlook on life; an outlook that draws direct correlation to the garden of life. The weed, historically a maligned part of the gardener's world, has eradication-inspired products galore to fill the shelves of the nearby garden center. The average gardener spends as much time taming the intrusive beings as he or she does pruning the intentional portion of the garden. It is in the process of the weeding that the gardener learns the intricacies of her or his garden.

The balance between the intentional and the unintentional is a larger by-product of life. In each life, "weeds" will come up among the crops and threaten to destroy and rob the true joy that life holds. It is through the "weeds" that character is built and that we learn to enjoy the other, intentional, planned events. Without the "weeds" to draw us closer to the important aspects of life, as they do in the garden, the things that we cannot observe from an upright view cannot come into clear focus. By examining our lives as a result of the "weeds", we are allowed to concentrate on the pruning of character. Each of us needs to concentrate on character to achieve the best on this side of heaven that we can.

The level of intimacy and balance achieved in the garden is a result of the weeds that bring us close to the soil, to the source, as they are pruned out. The weeds found in the common garden are resilient and invasive, as are the "weeds" that are not eradicated from the human experience. The weed, if broken into smaller pieces and allowed to remain in the soil will, like the Crown of Thorns Starfish, duplicate itself many times over and tear down the vital life that sustains the reef or the soil. The weeds should be pulled by the root to truly be eradicated from both the actual garden as well as in the garden of life or they will send the strength to the roots and take over the spirit. It is for this reason that I believe *she has returned.* Weeds that are lopped off but not pulled have a way of creeping back into everyday life to tarnish self-esteem or the focus on what is, in fact, important.

It is, in fact, the weed and the hours of careful pruning that first provided me with the peaceful time to draw from the earth the life lessons that this book is based on. The time set aside for gardening, is the time that allowed for my spirit to open to the wonders available if I listen quietly enough. It is the pruning process in the garden of my life which brought *her* back into my life and began my journey of writing these stories.

When a gardener tends...he is reborn.
\- Justin Matott

MY GARDEN VISITS

VIGNETTE ONE

Alchemilla mollis *(botanical name)* **Lady's-mantle** *(common name): Lady's-mantle will grow to two feet and will spread throughout the garden. The flower that it produces is a pale yellow against the silver of the surrounding leaves. It will grow well either in sun or in partial shade and prefers well composted soil. Lady's-mantle blooms in the spring and in late summer providing interest to border gardens and mixed beds.*

My father would joke with her about the name of the plant that he grew near the back patio of my childhood home. They would often kid each other about things of Old English lifestyle. They would speak of the Queen's coming for tea and that the Lady's-mantle would grace the dinner table and frame the other flowers in a spray of glorious color.

She came again to me as I knelt in the garden. With great care, I pulled creeping veronica away from a growing mass of bind weed. I prepared to yank out the intruder that would surely rob the delicate blooms of nutrient and would eventually choke away beauty from the small plant it planned to encase. Next to my hand was the eccentric spreading lady's-mantle. Everywhere else in my garden, I had to diligently tend to assure that nothing would be stifled or choked out by another flowering plant or a weed. The lady's-mantle was unique in the fact that it seemed to "own" the soil it grew from and the soil surrounding it. In retrospect, I realize it was a symbol, an example of how she had been...part of the garden, a member of the whole, yet unique and apart in her own way "owning" the space which she had inhabited.

The sky was an uneven gray and late summer evening orange mixture. The darker clouds threatened to release their moisture. The change in the sky ushered in quickly and had peculiarly invaded the usual comfortable, calm and warm summer evening. An abrupt cold snap rushed through the garden, one which seemed borrowed from the autumnal months, then it was gone. This summer had by all accounts begun strangely. An odd strain surrounded my life in a time that most people would envy, and I jokingly referred to it as the "halcyon days of summer." I was in a time of success regarding both my personal and my professional life.

She entered gently, to allow me a few moments to adjust to this experience without immediately jumping to the conclusion that I was obviously losing my reason. She seemed to be there to develop an area in my life that had, as yet, been incomplete. The balance of perspective, the reflection on a life now done would allow for the perspective of priority. I knew that I was in store for an experience which would deepen and widen my life. She was going to gently open a door in my heart that was in need of reflection. She had been sent to deliver a message.

It had been five years since I last held my mother's hand or felt her breath as I leaned down to kiss her one last time. It was with tears and regret and, extraordinarily enough, joy for her when I said "good-bye". That was the last time I saw her physically. She never really left me, (parents never really do), and I suppose it is impossible, as hard as we try to push away and find our independence, to really lose them. She, in so many ways both good and bad, had left her indelible imprint on my life. By all accounts, she was unique and eccentric. I remember many times my anger against her would well up so much that I wanted to harm her. Some of the turbulent years of my teenage experience had caused a gap between us. If we had not developed such a strong relationship as "friends" in my earlier years, I am now convinced that those years would have been much harder on me and her too. Even when I was pushing away to establish my own independence, the security of knowing she would be there was comforting. We spent several years locking horns over almost every issue. She consistently pushed me to communicate my frustrations and welling anger with her, and she could often dispel some of those feelings that the combination of my hormones, and my need to establish my own individual identity were causing me. My love for her would return in time to remind me of the frailties of the human being and the expectations that we put on one another.

I looked up and sensed that there had been a dramatic change in my garden. A presence, if you will. I know that these things leave most people wondering and skeptical and often times doubting the reality or relevance these events have in our lives. I looked across the various perennials and annuals that fill my garden and subconsciously accounted for the many hours which I had spent here. Sprays of multi-colored creeping sedums, daisies, columbines, pansies and low growing ground-covers dotted the landscape. The iris stood proudly above all of the other plants, with the splendors of magenta, peach and violet, deep yellow, and the multicolored scarlet and gold iris my children innocently referred to as "root beer." The slight breeze seemed to come to a complete halt as the presence of a soul, now gone, entered the dimension of my limited human imagination and crossed into my reality. I shuddered, though not from fear or cold, but from a realization that something larger than life and also extraordinarily familiar to me had entered "my reality."

The yard and gardens of my "seasons of experience" with her wrapped around my home, climbing fences, climbing the side of the house, stretching over into the fields behind the yard. Every inch of land I could dedicate to my passion, I had. The variety of plantings ranged from low creeping ground covers, which simply covered the hard to maintain areas, to plots of copious color and variety. Elaborate moss rock, aspens, hundreds of pansies, iris, columbines and multitudinous other plantings that just seemed to need a home spotted my yard.

I am a collector. Seeds, cuttings, split perennials... you name it, I have found it a home. I have been tempted to rescue house plants on the curbs from the awaiting trash trucks, to nurse them back to health. Once I was jogging in town and sighted six small trees in a dumpster behind a store. After inspection, I determined that there was absolutely nothing wrong with the trees that some nutritious soil, food and care couldn't overcome. Those skinny trees that I planted in a prominent place in the front yard of our old house, now shade it well. They stretch at least twenty feet above the house and have added dramatically to its value and appearance. The gardens I have left as my family has grown have left an individual mark, one I couldn't replicate if I had too. I have never been able to follow much of a plan in my gardens. The only rule which I have tried to establish is to know the individuals enough to make sure that they won't be tucked away behind something else, and therefore, robbed of a place to show their glory. Even this has been a difficult task for me. I am far from the technical gardener who would write a manual on the how to's.

I have always perceived the garden as a place to create; a place to be free to express the urgings of the moments, or the building of a long term strategy such as planting something tall, so that in several years it will cover something which distracts from the appearance of the yard. This is much the same way an artist strikes each canvas differently. To the inexperienced, the garden can seem an ominous, scary place to venture. I have counseled friends in the past who were afraid to venture past the simple, uniform gardens that grace the covers of catalogs. Whenever I see a row of tulips spread apart uniformly at two and a half inches, I feel compelled to intervene, to explain that tulips should be bunched, not planted by ruler to border. I drive engineers crazy with the free forms, but I have found in my many ventures in God's natural gardens, that the free flow of color and the mixtures is what He prefers also.

I have always had a strong belief in the hereafter, but never as strongly as on a Halloween evening five years ago. I had spent the previous three days in the sterile environment of a hospital tending to her. She had slipped into a coma from complications of an extensive brain surgery that she had been expected to survive. She left us wondering for several days if she would ever return to us.

We came to the time when the decision, that no one ever wants to make, and could only make out of the complete love and respect for the person's wishes, had to be made. As the most responsible and able member of the family, it was my, the youngest son's duty, to inform the doctors and nurses that it was time to allow her to go. It was time for her to rest and to meet her Creator. The Creator that she, like most frail humans, had spent the better part of her life wrestling with and trying to comprehend the enormous complexities of. When she slipped away it was without pain, without fanfare. Her body, exhausted and ready, let her go. Her earthly body lay limp as she left. The pain that remained was for the people who would go on without her love and friendship; those of us whom she would live within for the rest of our days on earth. She would live on in the eternal souls of those that crossed her path in significant ways, as will all of us, making it so important that the influence that lives on is positive.

I drove home alone that night, that chillingly cold, cruel Halloween evening. I cried and asked God why a person so young had to face life without a mother. She had been a confidant, a believer, the one that no matter who or what I was becoming, would remain proud of me and forever stay in my corner. She was gone. The hard reality crashed around me the way the waves engulf the coral and threaten to demolish it. The balance between going on and losing the departed loved one is confusing. It has taken me years to fully digest the fact that she is truly gone.

As I lay in my bed that night, the picture of a house with pillars at the front came to mind. I envisioned the pillars holding up the foundation, but one pillar was missing. I realized I was the house and she had been a crucial pillar in my foundation. I crept between sleep and sleeplessness for hours. Sometime after midnight, I awakened slowly, but totally. I was soon confronted with the reality that she was sitting on my bed, as she had so many times when I was a little boy, when lightning or a noise would scare me and I would call out for her. She was there as physically as she had ever been, but she communicated to me in a nonverbal, low cerebral manner that went beyond the normal human connection. She had come to reassure me that she was fine and she would now be in a place where her pain and the issues of human reality were no more. There was no eerie cloud or glow, no fanfare or ghostly apparition. As quickly as she came she left again. The experience left me with the terrible fear that I was losing my mind. I know to this day that this was no dream, no trick of my own mind to comfort me and allow me to fool myself into believing all was okay. No, she had been there and she had come to leave me with peace.

It was now almost five years later and she had come again to me in my garden. As my hand slipped away from the wilting bindweed, I continued to take in the panorama of my garden. Impressed with the fact that a garden takes on a whole new life when viewed at only three feet, as opposed to the outlook at an adult height, I realized that my children's world at six and eight was a totally different one than I was now experiencing. I remembered a time not too long before, when I returned to the backyard garden of my youth. I found myself surprised at the fact that it was not the size of a soccer field, as I had remembered it, but was really fairly modest in size.

The inevitable changes of life flashed about me. I returned to my weeding. Her presence grew stronger and I turned to see who was watching me. I could feel the piercing of her eyes and realized that I was being observed. As I released myself from my crouching position and took note of a small robin on the opposite side of my perennial border searching for a worm, I was at once, calmly aware of her presence. I was slightly bewildered and overcome by the fact that my mother had entered my garden through some channel I had yet to understand. She was now communicating to me in the same manner that she had the night she visited me and reassured me of her life going on in another dimension as mine must here.

"Mom?" I searched the garden, expecting to see her. She was not there, yet she was fully there. I could feel her communication. My eyes welled up and filled to the point that the moisture spilled across my cheek as the darkening clouds were threatening to do the same. I longed for her hug of reassurance that she had given me as a child. Though there was no physical touch, I was surrounded by the warmth and mothering which I had begun to forget. I knelt down and covered my face in the fear that my grief and vulnerability would be apparent to anyone who saw me speaking to the surrounding air. The earthy smell of the rich soil surrounded me. The clouds opened up and the large drops of an early summer rain pelted the garden and me softly.

"I am proud of you." Simple and relevant, this is what she had come to say to me this time. She came to forewarn me, possibly, of an oncoming storm and a time soon that I would be challenged to step up to some of life's hard times and be the man that she had raised, the man that she had purposely been hard on at times when the character could bend in one of two ways. In my youth, I simply thought she was cruel because she was not willing to bail me out of situations as my friend's parents did. She saw in me a weakness, a willingness to quit if allowed to, and she would have none of it. As I write this story, I realize it is as much about myself and my growing character which has taken on a whole lot of her even after she departed.

She left me again, but this time with a permanent change. I was no longer questioning the ongoing dilemma with which so many of us wrestle; whether or not there is life ongoing. I now know with certainty that if we are allowed to step outside of our box and listen calmly to our souls, we can find comfort in our incredible Creator and the wonders that lie in store for those that are open to it. I knew, in time, the memory of this meeting would begin to slip and I, like all adults that have forgotten the lessons of Peter Pan, would begin to doubt the wonders of this communication.

As I lay in bed a few nights later, I remembered our garden meeting and contemplated the whole reason she was once again visiting me. What was in store? Why had she come? What did it mean? Was I being prepared for something? Or was she simply coming back to reassure me that I had become, in the few years since she left, the man that she had purposed me to be?

VIGNETTE TWO

Myosotis scorpioides (botanical name) **Forget-me-not** (common name): The Forget-me-not grows up to twelve inches in height. It spreads in a low mounding habit and prefers fertile, moist, composted soil. It will grow well in sun or partial shade. Provides beautiful, early spring flowers and is propagated by root division or seed. The small blue/purple flowers with yellow centers grow in clusters and create a thick bed of color. They are very resilient and spread well and are best when massed in flower beds, used in border gardens, walkways, and other areas of the yard where low spreading flowers work well in contrast to taller plantings.

The Forget-me-not is a favorite in my borders. The masses of color in the spring are stunning, and when mixed with the later blooming tulips and daffodils, add beauty to the front of the house. The Forget-me-nots of my childhood home grew in a strange part of the yard...the nagging place every gardener wrestles with what to do...the place that really isn't evident to anyone else but the master of the yard. In that place was one of my mother's getaways. I would often see her reading or grading papers in a comfortable chair among the flowers.

It was early in the spring. Just a few weeks before the grape hyacinth, crocus, tulips, daffodils and other emerging bulbs would grace the snowy landscape with color. There is usually a short pause between the bulbs and new color in my yard. It is the early bulbs which provide the creative urges to once again treat my yard as an easel and to hasten to the local garden center to look over the new additions and plan for the warmer months to come. It is always difficult to go into the greenhouses where large tomato plants already have brought forth the delicate yellow blooms soon to be replaced, months in advance, with savory beefsteak tomatoes for someone luckier than me; someone with either the interior climate control and direct sunlight, or a greenhouse, that can make these early beauties flourish.

The earth was waking up, the soil beginning to retain the heat. Soon the soil would struggle against the sun and the other elements that had worked for eons to compact and/or break it down. As I turned the soil in the vegetable gardens, and readied my hanging pots for their colorful debut, I felt something mysterious happening. Fleeting thoughts and objects invaded my daily activities. It was as if a door to another dimension had opened and anything was possible as a result.

If I didn't know my mind so well, I would have simply assumed that I was going crazy. An example of what I am talking about is a little frog that sits in the birdbath. He is a blue-green little sculpted metal piece.

Logically I know that he is no more than that, but I could have sworn the little guy chirped and adjusted his stance. I have seen too many movies I guess, but maybe the otherwise normal conditions of life *do* change when the dimension changes to allow for a visit. I have experienced a series of extraordinary events since the first night she visited; since the day she left earth to go unencumbered by the weighty humanness with which we are saddled here, to float above the routine existence of the mortal condition. I had discounted the total relevance of her visit until she came back again. Since my first garden visit with her, the frequency increased. I have allowed myself to believe that it is possible to touch the other side and to consent to the unexplained.

I was startled to realize she had come back. Standing near the small teak bench and pulling off my rubber boots, I sensed her standing there in the back of the garden. She watched me for some time before she allowed me to know she was there. She communicated once again in her, (now becoming familiar), nonverbal way. She let me know that she was just there to observe me, and again, I sensed, to prepare me for something thus far unexplained.

Several carrots had over-wintered in the heavily composted and mulched soil of the garden. As I turned the earth with my hand to ferret out a carrot, I noticed a wholly intact avocado seed. With very little tarnish it had survived the composter with its high temperature and the weathering which had broken down the surrounding dirt. I washed the carrot off with the stiff hose. Other than a slight woodiness to the texture, it was a pretty good carrot. I imagined the taste of snap peas and the radishy flavor of the European lettuce I would put between the rows to hold down the weeds and provide variety to our daily salads.

My Mother loved sweet peas. They would climb along the fence in the yard and grow tall as their tendrils reached for all they could cling to. The wonderful sweet smell that would emanate from the wall of climbing color added such a calming natural environment to the early days of the garden. As a tribute to her, I decided to plant sweet peas every year thereafter. It is amazing how many meaningful events of our childhood, that brought so much enjoyment in the past, are forgotten or get clouded by our busy lives. I planted regular podded peas for eating. It is the usual tradition in my family to join together in the vegetable garden on warm summer nights to eat the small peas straight from the vines. They rarely make it to the kitchen except to be snapped in half and then sprinkled into salads and eaten by the fist-full. I often pull back the string and marvel at the small tender peas within the succulent pods. Each pea has the genetic make up to reproduce itself. The magic of the garden becomes intoxicating if one just takes the time to examine its intricacies and wonders.

Near the back of the vegetable garden lay a patchwork of little tender plants. It took me time to identify them. I won't dig out anything until I can prove it is neither beneficial nor wanted. I say this because if one has the time and the patience, one can actually domesticate some varieties of weeds. They add interest and beauty to an otherwise sterile bed of flowers. One spring, I learned the hard way not to weed through the garden with little knowledge. I found that I had eradicated nearly one hundred small columbines that were emerging from seeds which I had dutifully collected the previous summer from the mountains surrounding Vail. The few that were spared from my clumsy fingers became some of the most beautiful rare varieties I have seen. I wished for their color and for the entire beautiful display that was in store if only I hadn't "weeded" so hastily. Now I had to rely on the seeds, from the few which I had "accidentally" spared, to replenish the rest of the garden.

So many gardeners, with little imagination or desire to create, arrange their flower beds in rows staggered apart at similar, if not perfected, intervals. Life is too short to stand in a line and to conform to the next guy's plan. A garden requires its own signature. Back to the little plants in the back, I jogged my memory and recalled the last fall. On the day she first visited my garden, I sprinkled some pansy seeds around. The diminutive results pushed their way through the soil. I had purposely planted them in the back of the vegetable garden because of the rich, black soil which would provide them a good start. Then I would transplant them around the yard where a low lying spray of color would define some of the barren places still left ungroomed.

It seemed the complications of my busy life were preventing me from seeing clearly the needs around me. She seemed to be saying that I should take time to view the garden of life around me more carefully. That I should view my life in the same way I took in the new lives and wonders spreading forth in the gardens around my home. As I examined and very carefully thinned the small pansies so they would not choke one another out, she impressed upon me the need to make myself sensitive to those around me, especially my young and impressionable children.

A large spreading display of forget-me-nots grew together across the lawn from where I stood. She seemed to be motioning to me to move the teak bench to the spot under a small blue spruce yearning to shade me and the bench. The place provided privacy from any intruders and a refuge from the rest of the yard's activities. After I moved the bench and started spending time there, I found the creative urges growing. When I wrote there, it seemed easier to cultivate my thoughts. An additional benefit was that it became a safe haven for my children to crawl into my lap and snuggle on cool mornings or warm evenings, and provided the time to assure that I would not forget the meaning of relationships. The time with the little loved ones in our lives is so very important to savor and hold close. The little ones yearn to be noticed and to be lingered with by the so-important adults in their lives. These are the memories that my children will have of their father's garden. Memories that I hope and pray they have taken into their hearts and will, in turn, give to their children in the years to come. "Forget-me-not," she seemed to be saying...and I never would.

VIGNETTE THREE

Viola tricolor *(botanical name)* **Pansy** *(common name): The Pansy will grow to eight inches in height in small spreading mounds. The flower's markings resemble the characteristics of the human face. The Pansy prefers moist, fertile and composted soil. They do quite well in full sun or partial shade.*

The Pansy is a beautiful addition to any garden. My mother would take the whiskered blossoms and float them in a large, clear-glass vase on the kitchen table. There were always cut flowers in my childhood home and the Pansy was one of her favorites. In my father's gardens and in mine, there is plenty of room for resilient and beautiful Pansies.

I spent the better part of the evening in the front garden pinching back pansies. The heat of summer was coming on strong now, but the pansies preferred the cooler spring nights. If not pinched back, they would become very leggy and out of control. I find when I take the time to examine and prune them, they provide mounds of ongoing color. If you leave just a few spent flowers alone, they will produce large bulbs bursting with seed to allow for propagation in other parts of the garden. This was the time to give them as much nutrient and care as possible to assure long stands of color across the front of the porch way. In particularly warm portions of the winter, the hardy purple and yellow mixed mounds that nestle to the house for warmth would show through and bloom. Interesting, that in school yards across the country, children mockingly call one another "Pansy" as an insult to their supposed, blooming machismo.

The secret to a glowing garden is the constant care and pruning, and pansies are no exception. The beauty of the bloom, although prolific, is short lived and soon each blossom is replaced by another if the gardener cares enough to pinch off the fading blooms and keep moist compost around their bases. The loving attention is similar in nature to what a child requires to be secure and blossom into the best adult he or she can become. My goal was to carefully cultivate the small, young ones in my life, and to assure that it was with gentle hands that I weeded, disciplined and loved. To prune out too much would surely leave an empty gap where something not as beautiful would have taken over and spread. Just enough pruning would assure that the full beauty could take its course.

She entered the garden and observed quietly the care which I showed. I sensed there was a shift, a change, and I felt the familiar and extraordinary feeling of suspense. She communicated that I would need to show the same care to another loved one in the days near. I realized that she needed to communicate with me as much as I wanted the communication. In life, we had spent many hours speaking of issues deeper than most mothers will share with their sons. She was always willing to talk about the tough issues which make most parents squirm.

She and I had a strange bond when I was a child. In many ways I was a parent to her. She grew up in the depression, a first generation immigrant, the oldest of five children. She had left her homeland in Europe to come to the promises of America and the release from Hitler's hell that had just begun. She was a fascinating storyteller, and her tales of growing up in New York City during the depression were so alien to my youth in a small town in Colorado, that I always listened with great imagination and vivid pictures in my mind. She had a very hard childhood. She was forced to work when she was too young to do so, and then forced to raise her siblings because of a frail and sickly mother who died years before

I came to be. In many ways, my mother spent her adult life living out the youth that she had never had the chance to experience.

I remember a story that she told me one night at the dinner table. I was upset that we never had fish sticks like my friends' families did. She went on to tell a story of herself at twelve years of age begging on the streets for food because they were in the middle of the Depression and seven mouths needed to be fed. She would go to the neighborhood butcher and receive his week old fish sticks for free, and it was those that her family lived on for three years with very little other food for dinner to break the monotony. That was why we never did, and never would, eat a fish stick in her kitchen as long as the decision was hers.

She kept a jar of tartar sauce in the door of the refrigerator for years, unopened, and no one ever questioned why. I figure that it was the simple reminder to her of the years that her family had suffered. It was possibly her way of thumbing her nose at the fact that they wouldn't have even had the money to buy the seasonings then. The tarter sauce would have possibly made those awful, dry fish sticks of her time in the Depression bearable.

Since our first meeting in the garden, things have changed. I seem to see fleeting objects or fleeting presence more often now. Now that I realize there are other things than what the human eye acknowledges. I also realize that for the better part of my life I have been unconsciously aware of the fact that there is more to the dimension of reality than what most people live in day to day. It is strangely comforting to know there is something here with me because I believe that now I am open to it. It is a chance to unlock so many things which have baffled the imagination for years and are generally suppressed by our logical desire to compartmentalize everything into neat piles so that we can "understand them". The fact is few people have the opportunity to truly experience the fullness of reality outside of the "box". I now have no doubt, that she has returned to expand me to the fullness of the life experience.

When she left her earthly body, she was working on her third Masters degree. Why she needed to understand the DNA molecule after years of music theory and German and English teaching, I will never quite understand, and yet I guess in a way I do. There are few people who are willing to dream, to live life to the hilt. She was one of those rare people who saw life as God's gift to the explorer and she didn't want to be inhibited by the simple fact that it wasn't logical to pursue interests peculiar to most. One of the common comments made at her funeral, from people that had known her personally, was that she had lived a very full, rich life. The comfort they could take in her death was that she had lived her life more fully than most other people ever would. She had spent her "tour of duty" here relishing the flavors offered in life.

She impressed upon me in this visit that I needed to see to it that her beloved husband, my father, would take the same relish in his life now. He had viewed his life as empty since she left. She was one of those people that would fill the room with her presence, and when someone is like that, the downside for the person they live with daily is that they are usually in the shadows and their personality is more reserved and quiet. My father was now realizing that he had, for years, lived a great deal of his life through her energy, and now that she was gone, he must generate his own. This had been difficult for him to deal with, because he had come to rely on her. He viewed his life as an empty one now and was dealing with all of the feelings of grief and anger that he had, for so long, taken a back seat to her when he might have driven together alongside of her. Because I have taken on a lot of her characteristics, and in many ways have become with every passing year more and more like her, she seemed to be letting me know that it was her desire for me to work with my father and help him come into his own now. His future was once again an empty book waiting for the author to bring life to its pages, and to once again return to the journey and adventures which could be written in them. I committed to her that I would spend time with him and help him to come forth.

We all put away our grief in different ways. Some escape to vices such as alcohol, drugs and overeating; some work too much; others turn the rest of the potential pain inward and live the rest of their lives in silent suffering. The warmth and anguish of the memories of the past exist in the fibers of our everyday existence and will not release us until the day when we finally rest from these earthly suits and go home. She was like the pansy. It blooms during the coldest months, if given enough protection, and will provide color to any garden it graces. The pansy is resilient and strong, yet very delicate and requires care and proper environmental conditions to be its best.

VIGNETTE FOUR

Aquilegia *(botanical name)* **Columbine** *(common name): The Columbine will grow to heights of two to three feet and is a taller, upright and beautiful addition to any garden. They grow in a vast array of colors and in beautiful combinations of color. The species known to botanists and garden enthusiasts as A. caerulea is blue and white bicolor and is known best in paintings and flower arrangements. The Columbine is Colorado's state flower and grows in the meadows of the highlands freely. The Columbine prefers fertile, loamy soil in sun or partial shade.*

My children called them "granny's bonnets". The Columbine was her favorite flower, and it is mine also. She told me when I was a child, that since the Columbine was the state flower, you could go to jail for picking one. I know now that she just wanted to assure that her favorites, the blue and white ones that nestled against the aspen trees in the backyard, would remain pristine.

The morning she visited me again in the front gardens, I was celebrating my birthday by continuing my commitment to better health. I had run for just short of an hour and was returning to the house at the same time the sun was still coming up. I came to the front of the house and sat on the front porch. Examining the roses in the front bed, I beheld that some aphids were being farmed by the local ladybugs. A colony of black ants, farming these aphids like a farmer with his livestock, fascinated me when I realize the symbiosis between nature and itself. Several black ants were attacking a large ladybug driving her away from their precious "cows". I made a note to try an orange rind solution that I use to rid my trees of nagging beetle larva. It is a simple mixture of ground citrus rinds and water, fermented in the sun like a tea, then sprayed on the leaves. I refused to use the chemicals that drift and poison the small birds and other beneficial creatures that grace my gardens with their presence.

I stepped into the house and poured a hardy mug of cappuccino, then returned to the garden in the front of the house. Next to the porch, twelve large columbine plants waved in the slight, morning breeze. The tufts of red, purple, yellow, cream and scarlet, along with the three, red-twigged dogwoods and nankeen cherry trees, contrasted against the deep-green grass and cedar mulch. A lovely, orange hue blanketed the entire yard from the waking sun.

As I untied my shoes and stretched my aching thighs, she came and sat on the front porch swing behind me. She sat more quietly than I remember her. She had more commonly filled a room with her continuous laughter. I remember her best now in her later years, when I was an adult and we shared a friendship which would be enviable to most parent/child relationships. We were good friends and shared our hearts. Though she left too early, I know that I had more of a relationship with her than most men do in a long life of sharing experiences with their parents.

She would often dress with eccentricity. A plum-colored cashmere sweater, mustard-yellow sweat pants, white, high top tennis shoes, and the spirit of ten people festooned her when she would come to visit her grandchildren for the weekend. Our relationship had stabilized and was on an adult level. My wife helped considerably with that, and provided my mother with the daughter that she had always wanted. Before that our relationship was marked with the usual love/hate that every boy has for his mother as he struggles to attain freedom from a person he feels so much dependence on.

I crossed my legs, one over another, to get a full stretch in my hamstrings. My mind triggered a memory of a time when I was six or seven years old when several of the neighborhood children were taunting me and making fun of me because I didn't have a "real" mom. I recall that it hurt and confused me that the kids didn't consider that my mom was a real mom. I went home angry and bewildered that I was different from most kids because I had been adopted. I remember my mother telling me that the kids that were saying this were crazy...that I was doubly blessed because I had a birth mother who loved and cared so much for me, that she wanted a better life for me than she could provide...that I had a "real" mother who had sought me out because she couldn't have her own, and if she had been able to, she would have wanted them to be exactly like me. I remember the strange comfort and pride I felt from that day on. I was special, and no one else that I knew had two special women like that who cared for them so completely.

On my birthdays as a child, she would mention that there was a special woman thinking of me somewhere and wishing me the happiest birthday of anyone else. I remember thinking that my birth mother was probably baking a birthday cake and toasting me wherever I was. I never thought until I became a parent, how hard it would be to wonder, all those years, what had become of the child that she only met in passing in the bed where she gave him life. A true sacrifice for another. I believe God has a special reward for those mothers and fathers who made the decision to give the precious life to another. To allow adoptive parents to nurture and raise their child in an environment that they must have believed would provide the life they would have chosen. The life that would be forever in place of the life that they could provide, whether out of circumstances or personal choices. I now toast my birth mother on each of my birthdays, and pray one day that I will be able to thank her personally for her sacrifice and her gift of life to me.

She seemingly had come this time to simply wish me a happy birthday and to remind me that I had two mothers; one I had loved so much, and the one that had loved me so totally that she had given me an ultimate birthday gift...the chance to attain all of the potential that I had. I lifted my mug of cappuccino to both of them and thanked God for them.

VIGNETTE FIVE

Iris hollandica (botanical name) Dutch Iris (common name): The Iris will grow to three feet preferring moist, fertile, composted soil. It grows well in sun or partial shade. These beauties are best when massed in flower beds and used as a tall, back of the border color addition in the early spring. The numerous colors and variety of this rhizome allow the gardener to use it in abundance throughout the garden. In the later months long after it has ceased blooming, the tall bladed leaves add texture and interest to the borders of my gardens.

My father is actually the one that gifted me as a child with a love for the soil. He would grow numerous varieties and colors of Irises. The house of my childhood was surrounded by tall dappled Irises and my border gardens still hold the descendants of his legacy, as do many of my friends' gardens with whom I have shared his original bounty. My mother would decorate the house in the spring with the tall bunches of Irises and the whole house would smell of their grapey sweetness.

Small purple Japanese Iris and spiderwort speckle the quickly sloping hill leading around the east side of my yard. It was a very difficult part of my garden to plan because it has such a dramatic slope that the water runs off of the soil easily. It seemed no matter how much I amended the soil, it still didn't accomplished my desires. I was tempted to allow creeping sedum to take over the entire area, but to do so would be to admit defeat. It would be like a painter that became frustrated from trying to accomplish a certain look on a canvas resorting to painting the same small design over and over with little color or style variance. I continued to add humus and to find plantings which spread not only above the ground, but below the soil to establish it.

Already wilting and fading were the Dutch Iris, which are one of my favorites. I treasure one of the iris in particular because of the pleasant connotation it brings. Like those smells, tastes, and sights that take you back to a time in the past. Whenever I am in an old hotel's lobby, the mixture of age, cigar smoke and, I assume, mildew, has a way of taking me back to a time when I was very young and my parents took my brother and me to stay in a historic hotel. I remember a very comforting feeling staying there, and remember vowing that I would live in an old hotel when I was an adult. When I enter an old hotel, and the multiple smells mixed together over many years hit my nose, I am back there almost in a physical way. This is what the deep red and yellow irises do to me. I have always liked them because they were my junior high and high school colors. My father had many of them in his gardens. As a child, I would gather great bouquets for my mother to put on the dining room table.

The Dutch Iris is a larger, more sturdy variety than the Japanese Iris. The Japanese Iris is similar to one I see every so often in the mountains outside of Breckenridge. There is a valley close to Georgia Pass which is slightly marshy and has a nice spotty blanket of summer wildflowers. In the middle of all of the other common wildflowers is a stand of wild iris. The deep purple sticks out and can be observed from twenty feet away on the dirt road. If it weren't for the integrity I learned as a child, I would rob the natural habitat of it's bounty and they would be resting in my garden now.

A composite of crushed, red rock wound down a curving slope. Terracing it and slowing the hill was a series of railroad ties on my difficult side of the gardens. I was adding some brick to the composite to experiment with the walkway to see if it would slow the speed at which the lawn mower traveled the path. She sat on the pile of bricks watching me. She seemed to have come to find out about the children, my children, her grandchildren. My boys busied themselves in the backyard with a hose and made threats that if I didn't join them by my own free will, they would be including me anyway. I knelt down and picked through some of the foliage around a group of iris and shred a few wilted leaves into pieces. As I pushed the leaves into the composted soil at the base of the iris, a spray of water overtook me and shocked me back to my seat. The boys howled with gleeful laughter and ran around the corner of the house. She watched intently, and I knew that I must leave her to defend my honor with the lads. As they began to inch toward the side of the house, I stepped into a culvert next to the house and waited. I picked up a watering can, and as my oldest stepped around the corner, I let him have it.

After twenty minutes of water play, I returned to the spot to the east. I realized she was still there, yet she was between the two places, where she lived now and where I lived. I felt a sense of confusion. An odd crispness in the air reminded me of the last few weeks in September when the air takes on a strange thinness and seems to drop ten degrees overnight. A mixed feeling always overcomes me when this happens. A certain peace and a longing collide in me when I realize that this snap in the air is signaling the autumn and eventually the winter. It will replace the warm evenings of summer. Winter will once again come causing the hibernation of the beauty on earth that will wait to burst forth again in an array of early spring color.

This time she had no direct purpose in her communication, but seemed to have a longing to be near her grandchildren. They were oblivious to her presence, but she was intent on watching them and seemed to be pleased to hear their laughter and see them growing into little men. She looked at my youngest son with a great deal of curiosity and seemed to be saying that he was the same as I was as a child. I have had a great many comments about how much he is like me. She seemed to be at peace about them, and I took it to mean that all was well and that she approved of who they were becoming. It is my youngest that has no recollection of her. She had spent hours looking at him and cooing to him when he was just an infant, but it was in his second autumn that she was taken from us, so of course he didn't know her. He spoke of her with tenderness and affection that he learned from his older brother who did know her, but as time passed, also struggled to reconstruct her in his memories.

Interesting...the way the circle of families and relationships with one another reconstructs itself constantly. Every so often, I will see something in my children that reminds me of her, only to realize that it is probably a trait I too possess which they have taken on. One wonders how far it goes back. From whom did she draw the personality traits and from whom did that ancestor, and so on it goes.

I weeded around the small, strawberry garden positioned below a red brick wall that my wife and I built the previous fall. She stood peering around the back of the house. For the first time, I realized that she was not the same at all as she was when she was here. At least she was not the same as the mother I remembered. I imagine that her present image was a closer reflection of the one that she possessed when she was a much younger woman. The face and body she had before the numerous casualties, both large and small, that she attained in life ravaged her body. Interesting to me that she really didn't have a physical shape the way we might imagine, but yet somehow, in a more deep sense, I know what she looks like. It is hard to describe what these communications are truly like. I think of movies I have seen where the central character is the only one that can see the apparition and the others think he or she is crazy.

She sat and gazed at my boys at play for some time while I puttered about the garden. I was intent on what I was doing and, milling from the work shop in the garage to the side yard, I realized that she had gone again. My oldest son left his little brother in play and walked over to me, plopping down in my lap. Throwing me off guard, we both collapsed to the ground. His eyes teary, he hugged my neck and said, "Daddy, I miss Grandma."

"Forget-me-not," she seemed to be saying
...and I never would.

VIGNETTE SIX

Helianthus annuus *(botanical name)* **Sunflower** *(common name): The Sunflower grows to eight feet or slightly higher depending on the variety. It stands upright and will form a large, orange-yellow and nut-brown flower atop leafy stalks. As the head heavies itself with seeds, it will turn to the ground as if to prepare to ensure its survival by repropagation. It thrives best when given full sun and well drained soil. Varieties of the Sunflower boast the largest flowers in the plant world.*

She loved art, music, paintings, literature, museums, architecture, and anything that required creativity on the part of the human and allowed what is best about him to show forth. The paintings of Sunflowers by Van Gogh and others decorated the walls of my childhood home. I remember many times how she would tell me that they did not do justice to the originals which she had spent hours studying in her many trips back to the European continent she had loved so dearly.

The little mouse nibbled nightly on the drying sunflower seed heads. I found piles of discarded shells on the shelf and floor of my shed. I had considered numerous times the thought of a trap, but I find myself wondering if the little brown mouse was just storing her nest for the tough weather which lay ahead, and quite possibly, she was feeding other little furry heads. Store bought sunflower seeds are cheap and actually taste better than those anyway, so I made the decision that I would leave that section to her. If she invaded my flower seed banks it would be another story entirely.

I planted the sunflowers against the back fence where they received full sunlight. I find it curious the way they shoot up six to eight feet and develop their single flower that brings forth the bounty for nature's little creatures. The sunflower has always reminded me of the lion...the way it overlooks the surrounding territory with an exalted view. It has bold colors that stand out against the rest of the garden. I loaded the bird feeders several times and, in my own anthropomorphic way, believed the birds and now the mice appreciated me and think of the good fortune they have at the hands of this caring gardener. The shed is a quiet place, a place to putter and replant and file away the numerous seeds that I collect on my journeys. I had gotten some dandies the last time my family went to Vail, when carefully and secretly we picked off pansy and columbine seed heads.

My mother must have been in the shed that morning, because although I hadn't "spoken" to her in the garden for some time, I knew she had been here. I went into the shed to retrieve a trowel and the super phosphate which nourishes the dahlia tubers which lie inches under heavily composted soil in the back of the borders and would provide, once again, the incredible flowers the size of a dinner plate. She was a Leo and so am I. Although we never held any stock in the signs of the heavens, we would joke about the fact that one house was too small for two Leos. The king of the jungle is generally very territorial and neither of us were an exception.

I stood in the shed for what seemed like an hour waiting for her to "speak". The heat was intense. I drifted in and out of thoughts of my childhood, of the house in the country that was my home. Her presence assured me again that she was in a better place. She was no longer suffering the pain of life and the burden of a body which would constantly betray her brilliant mind. Memories came flooding in with vivid recollection; a time when I was in the backyard jumping on the trampoline when I heard loud shouting coming from the kitchen and the breaking of precious clay. I ran from the backyard to find her standing in the kitchen in a rage over something not articulated, except for the fact that she was throwing antique bone china at the wall. These times were so irrational and frequent for several years. She would go into fits of rage over seemingly trivial issues and destroy things she held precious, including, possibly unbeknownst to her, her son's confidence and security. I held her arms as she attempted to end the life of another antique dinner plate. She slumped to the floor and began to cry and hold her head as though it would explode if she didn't. The headaches and the dizziness made her so volatile. When she lost the hearing in her ear and the headaches continued with such regularity, we all became perplexed. The sobbing would go on for hours, and I, (as a young boy), tried in vain to comfort her. The enormous confusion I felt was overwhelming. After her "spells" I would convince her to rest in her room upstairs and I would return to the kitchen and sweep away the evidence so my father would never know.

Once she got a new tomato-red Chevrolet Impala. I remember the neighbors coming over to examine and comment on the car. It was the first time she had bought a car that wasn't a Cadillac. Several days later she came rushing into the house in a panic. She ordered me to the car, but I protested because I was enjoying Gilligan's Island, (or was it the Green Hornet?), on the family's thirteen inch Sears black and white television. She insisted that I follow her to the car. When I got in, she shoved a brown paper bag in my face and told me to read the instructions. The bag contained two cans of red spray paint. She pulled the car onto the dirt road leading from our front yard to the wheat fields which rolled across the surrounding landscape. We got about three miles from the house and she came to an abrupt halt and ordered me out of the car. I was to cover up a large dent and scratches that she had managed to make on the driver's side of the car. She explained that if we painted it, my father would not notice the damage. I began to spray and soon realized that the paint was much more orange than the car. I tried to explain and she instructed me that it would change as it dried. I did a pretty good job and used both cans to mask the damage. We drove back over the dirt road to our house and when we got out of the car we both gasped at the sight! The side of the car was encased in a thick, reddish mud. When my father came home that night the first thing he said as he entered the front door was about what had happened to the *$#@! car.

Several months later came Halloween. As I readied to go trick or treating with my older brother, I realized that my mother was acting very strange. I saw that she was drinking a glass of wine and figured she had just had too much. Something about the way she was acting made me delay my departure. She sat in the living room with my father and several of their friends who had come for the night of haunting. I saw that they were all drinking and thought they were being somewhat silly for adults. Her eyes were peculiar and scared me. I watched as she began to slur her words and look dizzy. I asked her if I could help her, and she said that she was okay, that I should go out with the other kids and have fun. I parented her by asking her to stop drinking, to which she stated that she hadn't even had half of a glass of wine. I didn't believe her. She stood to go to the kitchen and fell straight onto her head and passed out. When she awakened several minutes later, she complained of a terrible headache and dizziness. We helped her to the couch. I left and stood behind the house crying for a long time before I joined my friends.

Several nights later she awoke in the middle of the night and headed for the stairs leading down to the kitchen. I awoke to a loud thudding noise and my father coming fast from their bedroom. She lay at the bottom of the stairs with a broken arm and a large gash across her face from hitting the opposing wall. My father, in his distress, admonished her for drinking too much. Several days later she was admitted to the hospital with a lemon sized tumor in her brain. Weeks after fourteen hours of surgery, she lay in the hospital debating with a doctor about how silly it was to listen to neurosurgeons speaking of tumors in terms of fruit and nuts when describing their sizes to patients. She was always a character. The tumor would eventually come back eleven years later and rob her of life and me of a mother and a dear friend.

"The sunflower has always reminded me of the lion...the way it overlooks the surrounding territory with an exalted view."

VIGNETTE SEVEN

Antirrhinum majus *(botanical name)* **Snapdragon** *(common name): The Snapdragon is a resilient annual which will grow to three feet in height. Take care to plant after the danger of frost has passed in fertile, composted soil. It will grow well in sun or partial shade. The Snapdragon will add an array of color when massed in flower beds and can be used as a tall back-of-the-border color addition in the summer. The colors range from yellow to red, pink, white, orange and bicolor. They are good for cuttings in flower arrangements, and will provide variety in plantings.*

My children could make the Snapdragons talk. This is a gift that God gives children, because as adults, our fingers become too cumbersome to manipulate the little Snapdragon mouths into the magical talking heads. I used to sit as a child in my father's garden and make the small dragons speak to one another and enter into imaginary wars. My mother would often observe me from her kitchen window as she went about preparing one of her magnificent gourmet dinners. I remember that I would pretend not to notice that she was watching me and I would show off to entertain her.

Standing in the backyard, I pulled several weeds away from the tender leaves of some emerging columbines underneath a Washington Hawthorn tree near the deck. When the Washington Hawthorn blooms it's tender white blossoms, it provides a huge bouquet of flowers next to the deck. In the fall it produces brilliant, carmine berries which attract numerous birds right to the deck for some intimate bird watching. I make a mental note to put several bird feeders on each of the outside posts of the deck to assure the birds of winter a meal when they rest here from their journeys. On the other two sides of the deck, I planted pear trees which were now peeking over the deck that is at least fifteen feet off of the ground. They too provide a fragrant bouquet when they bloom.

As I puttered below the deck, clearing the area of the little weed invaders, my nose caught the scent of a mellow gravy, possibly beef stroganoff or roulades from somewhere down the street, probably old lady Stroh's house. She, a lonely widow, was particularly kind to the neighborhood children. No one would leave her house without an armful of something savory or sweet. Gardening, cooking and baking were all her passions. With no family close, she had done a good job of adopting all of us as her "children". At Halloween she filled the children's sacks with several pounds of candy, baked goods, and a large, blueberry popcorn ball. Refreshing in this day and age that the children could still enjoy an old fashioned part of the trick-or-treating without us worrying that they shouldn't eat it. Mrs. Stroh particularly favored my children and asked me to pick up a small toy near Christmas that I knew they would like so she could "give them something that would have meaning". She allowed the children to cruise up and down between her numerous rows of raspberry and gooseberry thickets. I went down there that evening to sit on her front porch and rock on a comfortable old chair and partake in a delightful peach or raspberry cobbler, or some other delectable baked item. I would bring her yellow squash and some cucumbers from my vegetable gardens and, if the children had not picked the tomato barrels clean, I would bring her a bowl of fresh Roma tomatoes which she would in turn boil into a sauce. She had loved gardening for the better part of a century, but was finding it too hard to bend down to weed and harvest. She let the large back gardens go to berries which flourished in her rich composted soil.

It must have been the mellow smell that wafted through the yard that brought my mother to the garden this time. She had been such a wonderful cook. She had studied French at the Cordon Bleu in Paris, and had spent years reading cookbooks and honing her skills. Ours was a household filled with gourmet cooking, opera, classical music, books, art and a true European influence. My father was entrenched in the classics as well as the country lifestyle. I never understood how my father could so easily switch from Brahms to Hank Williams in the same morning. As an adult, I now understand that inspiration takes its own path if we are flexible and allow ourselves freedom of variety.

I finished the weeding near the deck and grabbed a cold soda from the little refrigerator which sat inside the basement door. It allowed me to quench my thirst without tracking into the house or having to perform the chore of removing my shoes. Then I retreated to the getaway that I had established in between the spruce and the lilacs where the forget-me-nots spread. I rested on the teak bench and admired the little, church bird house that my brother-in-law had made for our family as a house warming present. Under the bench was an odd assortment of things. I stooped down to observe. There in a hand-dug circle of soil and slowly decomposing pine needles rested a strange little assortment, comprised of wood shavings, small pine cones, acorns, matchbox cars, GI Joe's, some wilted snapdragon flower heads and drying poppy seed pods. It appeared as though the boys had been pretending that the snapdragons were some sort of enemy to the others, and a great war had taken place there earlier. I picked up a red flower head and pinched it between my fingers. The red blood from the flower oozed out staining my hand.

"Dad, what are you doing?!" My youngest son stood there, a great look of disgust on his face.

"What's this?" I ignored his impudence.

"Dad! That's the red alien dragon!!" He stamped his foot and seemed to be threatening my very life.

"Can I play?" I replied.

His demeanor changed immediately. "Okay, do you want to be the alien dragons or the Army guys?" It is such the nature of children to play. They long to have the adults in their lives enter into their lives where they are; to relate to their worlds, and not have to conform to the rules imposed by us. Whenever I spent time wrestling on the ground or just entering into their worlds, my wife would remark on how changed their behavior would be for days. She called it their "Daddy fix".

"I'll be the aliens," I said. It comforted me to see that the imagination of my children couldn't be completely snuffed out by the television or the other modern toys that cannot compare at all to the Legos or the Tinker toys of my boyhood. He hit my hand with a brittle poppy seed pod as he was aiming for the small acorn and snapdragon alien. I realized the seed pod was a crude spear and, after this war, we would be introducing the poppy to this part of the yard. No matter, it would be pretty. We played there in the shade for an hour, which of course as I stood to quit, was not enough time for my son. He wished for the game to go on for another hour.

She sat on the teak bench watching us interact and seemed to enjoy the way we had bonded. This time as I noticed her, it seemed that my young son was also aware of her presence. He crawled into my lap quickly and snuggled uncharacteristically close to me. The mighty warrior, the evil alien dragon master that had spent the last hour slaying unimaginable creatures, was afraid of this "ghost". I began to try to explain her to him when I suddenly realized that no explanation was necessary. He seemed to sense that I was very comforted by her presence and quickly dismissed it. He hopped down from my lap and walked the long way toward the grass from the teak bench and yelled for me to come and throw the football. I wasn't sure if he was simply changing the subject to avoid the situation because he was uncomfortable.

I yelled back that I would be there momentarily. I turned to where she was watching him play with our little mutt and told her that I really missed her. She seemed to be entranced with the way my son was so much the image of me, her once little boy. I never thought mortals would feel pain after death, (but then I never really believed it was possible to rejoin the earth after death), yet I sensed that she was longing for a time long ago when I would have crawled into her lap for comfort. I thought her "eyes" were flooded as mine were and that a strange sadness had overcome her that I had not seen before. I said again to her that I missed her and that the smell of the gourmet dinner cooking down the way reminded me so much of her.

She "spoke" to my heart telling me that I should continue to care for those who had few to care for them. She was proud of the way I paid attention to the little old lady down the street; that it is the desire of the Creator she was now in the presence of, to reach out and do His work on this sphere. I suddenly felt a lot like I was experiencing a similar ghost to the one of Marley speaking to Scrooge. I wondered as we spoke, if Dickens had such visitations as these; if it had in fact been a visitation which had inspired him to write the Christmas Carol.

She continued on the issue of God's desire for His human race to learn to love for the sake of love itself. The desire to pursue the purpose that God has for His people, which is to nurture, to care for one another, and to love the unloved. He has no greater calling that I could follow. I made a note to spend more time with Mrs. Stroh and the other Mrs. Strohs in my life; to give time and love to the people that I could touch, and to make sure my boys learned the value of caring. That night I rocked on Mrs. Stroh's old porch rocker and promised to mow her lawn the next morning.

VIGNETTE EIGHT

Papaver orientale (botanical name) **Oriental Poppy**
*(common name): The Oriental Poppy will grow three to four
feet and stands upright in the garden. It prefers moist,
fertile, composted soil and grows best in full sun. Generally
propagated by seed or root division, it blooms in spring and
in late summer. The Poppy adds an array of color with a
black center among orange, pink, red, white, purple and
other vibrant colors. The flowers are large atop long green
stems, and stand out when mixed in flower beds or used as
a tall, back-of-the-border, color addition in the early spring.*

A small creek burbled and boiled through the backyard of
my childhood home. The creek to me was a place to catch
crawdads and frogs, but as I recollect, it was also a
beautiful refuge for wild asparagus that we would collect for
our mother and then eat slathered in butter and lightly
salted. In addition to the asparagus, numerous colors and
varieties of Poppy grew there. Some thoughtful gardener,
probably my father, had broadcast seed to make the creek
banks come alive with vibrant colors of the daisies,
sunflowers and other wildflowers.. For years people would
marvel on the way the yard looked, and would come when
my father did his annual perennial separations. He would
lay them next to the old dirt road for all gardener "want-to-
be's" to begin their own plots with.

My family had just returned from Breckenridge. The cultivated flowers in the downtown area and the wild flowers dotting the mountains were in full bloom. I envy the way God gardens His hills and valleys. I've spent hours upon hours trying to achieve a particular look, and the mountains and nature seem to be so "easily" adorned with color and splendor. My garden, despite all the time that I cultivate and weed, does not compare to the way God has designed it in His nature.

As we walked around the main street section of Breckenridge, we were amazed at the incredible assortment of flowers and plantings. Numerous restaurants were covered with hanging baskets bursting with pansies, creeping phlox, geraniums and intensely colored groupings I could not identify. We received blank stares when we asked our waiter at the small place where we ate lunch, if he knew the identities of these little flowers. The poppies there were as large as a coffee saucer, and the intense orange reminded me of wet, circus peanut candies, their black centers, the watchful eyes on the garden.

In addition to the floral arrangements in the little village were numerous wildflowers in God's garden. As we hiked through a field several miles to a remote camping site, every color in the spectrum was present. It intrigues me that the "weeds" in God's garden take on a very different look than when they intrude in the domesticated garden, trying to reclaim the land that is their birthright.

There were some larkspur stands amongst a variety of other plants on the hills, and then every three feet or so a tall wild sunflower popped up and added a golden dimension to the purples, pinks, whites, greens and other softer muted colors the eye only registers if you are looking for them.

I jogged ahead of my family to scout out a new site, a place near the winding streams, remote enough to allow us privacy. I knelt down to examine a small flower that I could not identify and cursed myself for forgetting the little wildflower book which I usually carried with me when camping. She whispered, and I felt a confusion. I had never encountered her anywhere but in my own garden and in my own element. I looked up and searched the little valley for her. I knew she was there, but I couldn't find her. After searching up and down the green, grassy valley, I looked up into a tall spruce tree and she was seemingly perched upon a high bow. She probably had never climbed a tree in her life on earth, at least it had been many years since she would have.

My older brother and I had built a tree house out of pilfered, construction wood in a very large cottonwood tree across the creek and small gravel road from our backyard. The tree overlooked a pond and a large, grassy horse pasture surrounded by barbed wire. It was a magical place for me as a child, and a refuge from the obligatory family things when I was a teenager. My mother would call from the back door when dinner was ready, and the tree house gave a full view of the entire house so I could see who was coming and going. The tree house was quite large and had most of the creature comforts a child needs: carpeting, posters and a Playboy magazine that one of the boys had pilfered from his father. This provided us with hours of self-taught sex education.

My brother and I kept the tree house stocked with Big Hunk candy bars, Necco wafers, Pixie sticks, Sweet tarts, which then were the size of your hand, and bags of penny bubble gum that we would purchase at the *U-Pump-It* gas station or the Bait Shop several miles away near the main road. The pond the tree house overlooked, that we always called "the pump", was the reservoir for irrigation water for the entire area. My father was the "pump monitor", which meant that during the months of irrigation, his job was to prime the pump morning and night to assure the citizens of water for their gardens and lawns. The main reason he had taken on this job was because we lived at the top of the hill right across a gravel road from the pump.

One warm, summer night my brother and I got the brilliant idea that we would play a little trick on our father. We snuck down from the tree house and climbed the locked gate around dinnertime when most of the neighbors in the surrounding area were watering their parched lawns and gardens. We shut the pump down and quickly climbed back into the tree house. Almost instantly, without the constant droning of the pump with it's mechanical whirring, the songs of birds, frogs and crickets joined together in a chorus of sorts creating a symphony in the fields surrounding us. We could hear the phone begin to ring across the street in our house. It rang several times in a row and soon my father came out the back door and crossed the gravel road. He whistled and talked cheerfully to my dog who followed along behind him obediently. Unlocking the gate to the pond, he looked curiously at the pump, perplexed that the large wheel that turned the valve was turned to the "off" position. He cranked it open again, and reprimed the pump, locked the gate, crossed the road, and went back into the house.

We giggled and rolled around in the tree house at the way we had fooled him. Then we waited for a few minutes. When we thought the coast was clear, we shimmied back down the tree and back into the pump. We cranked it off again and quickly ran back to the tree and up into the tree house. Within minutes the phone began to ring again. He came bustling across the road, a little less patient this time, and the dog hurried along with him. He wrestled for the key and re-entered the pump. When he realized that the wheel was turned off again, he looked around and cursed the "smart alecks" that were "messing with him". My big brother and I smothered our giggles, afraid that he would hear us. Although we were quite high in the tree, we were only twenty feet or so away from him. My dog's ears perked up and looked up into the tree. We held our breath as our father looked around for the culprits.

He walked across the street with disgust, looking back every so often. He apparently didn't notice that my dog was still sitting beneath the tree wagging his tail. My big brother suppressed his own howl and held his other hand over my mouth since I was unable to keep my composure. We could see our father looking out the front glass window toward the pump, trying to hide behind the curtains in case the jokers that were tormenting him could see him. We rolled around laughing so hard that I thought we were both going to wet our pants and fall out of the tree.

After what seemed like an hour, we ventured back down, hugging the side of the tree opposite the road and our house. We snuck down to the far end of the pump and crawled under the fence where the tall weeds hid us from exposure. We crawled around the pond to the pump and silently turned it to the "off" position. This time we tried to hug the side of the slippery, mud wall opposite the tree, fearing that our father might be watching again and would spot us jumping the fence. I neared the back of the pond and suddenly my feet slipped out from under me. I started into the pond feet first. I reached for some weeds to keep from going in but ended up going in sideways, splashing my brother with muddy water and submerging myself completely. I came out of the water like a wet animal and sneaked under the fence scratching my bare back on the metal fence.

My brother cranked the pump shut, his laughter uncontrollable, and headed for the tree. By the time I got to the tree the phone began to ring again, and my back was smarting from the deep scratches. My brother was howling with laughter and pushed me aside, scrambling up into the tree house. I went to climb the tree, but my shoes were so wet they kept me from being able to address the first few feet of the tree. The phone rang again and I could hear my father cursing loudly. My brother was screaming with laughter, and I was trying to decide if I should abandon my tree climbing attempt. I froze to the side of the tree as I heard the screen door on our back porch slide open. There was no way now that I could make it up the tree without my father seeing me.

Instead of coming back across the street to the pump, my father came out on the back porch and called us in for dinner. He stood there with his hands on his hips and called again. My brother whispered loudly to me to answer him and, that if I gave him away, he would give me a pounding. I knew I was going to have to take the fall for this one. I went to my knees and then into an army crawl and tried to secret myself in the weeds as I slid down into the ditch. I crawled below the ditch line in the rushing irrigation water about twenty feet toward the house, creeping along in the muddy water, fearing that the slick, muddy bottom and sides would pull me in and drench me. My legs burned as I pushed my hunched-over form along to avoid detection before I was so obviously far from the tree house, that I couldn't possibly have anything to do with the mischief. I popped up when I thought it would be obvious that I was nowhere near the pump, and was merely catching crawdads. What I hadn't counted on was that Frisky, my little beloved mutt, had been following me along the ditch leading my father directly above me. My brother snickered in the tree house as he watched the whole production taking place. My father usually had a good sense of humor about him, but this time, apparently, we had pushed him too far. He sent me to bed, sun still up, without any supper. Later when he had gone out to work his garden in the cool evening hours, my mother knocked on my bedroom door. She came in with a snack and stroked my head to assure me that I was still loved.

Another time in that tree house, possibly during the same summer, my brother and I did something that, to this day, I still remember with a certain shudder and a strange tightening in the back of my throat. My big brother and I had both developed a taste for the finer things from our mother, and one thing that we shared totally, was a love for the taste of real butter. Our parents kept a large freezer in the garage to house the enormous cache of food which kept my mother's gourmet kitchen alive with flavors and new dishes, as well as keeping her growing boys well fed. One of the reserves kept there in abundance were large blocks of butter. One summer morning my brother and I decided to steal a pound of butter from the freezer and snuck across the street with it. We gleefully climbed the tree house, our mouths watering as we anticipated this secreted and delightful indulgence. I remember we both had an army pocket knife which we used to cut off generous portions of the butter, and with it still half frozen, proceeded to eat the butter by the mouthful. We giggled and enjoyed the bounty of our stolen loot.

We must have gotten about halfway through the pound of pure butter when we both started to tire of the taste, and we figured it was because we were eating it without the grace of any bread. We climbed down the tree house steps and ran across the street, back to the freezer, and found a plump loaf of dark pumpernickel bread. We snuck the bread up into the tree house and in the time we were gone, the butter had begun to melt making it easy to spread on the delicious, but half-frozen bread. We slathered it thick on the bread and gobbled it down. The greasy experience started to turn our young stomachs. We had enjoyed the taste of butter so much on our mother's various dishes, that we challenged each other to continue until the pound of butter all but disappeared. I don't remember who lost their butter first, but I do remember we both did before we could get back out of the tree. I couldn't touch the stuff for years after. I still use butter very sparingly and eat my pumpernickel bread dry. Whenever I see someone slathering it on an ear of corn or piling it on bread, I remember the summer day when my love affair with butter ended in a tree house with my big brother.

Much later in that same tree house, I would have my first encounter with a "real girl", not just the pictures that we boys had worn thin with our naive stares and our mock kisses as we grew older. She was three years older than I was, which of course provided her with the right amount of experience for a young man, who at that point had kissed only his mother and his dog. She was rumored to have "French-kissed", and on that rainy day in the tree house, I joined the club of "French-kissers". After discovering partially the true meaning of the differences and the relationship between the sexes, I climbed down the tree and slid under the fence to the pond to catch frogs with a strange new sensation and a tickle in my stomach. From the pond, I could hear her teaching one of my buddies the technique of the French. I wasn't sure if the jealousy I felt was because she was kissing another boy, or that he was not there with me crawling around in the mud catching frogs and crawdads.

My family caught up with me in the meadow that I had been scouting out for the camping space. The children began to complain that they were lugging so much stuff, while I was "just sitting under a tree relaxing". I looked up into the tall spruce. She seemed to be smiling and reveling in the fact that I had discovered once again the joy of my childhood. Because of this, I would surely focus on the childhood of my own children.

My mother impressed upon me that the memories of my childhood in the country were a real gift. One that had made me the man I am, and that I should be very thankful for them. She also wanted me to make sure my own children were provided the opportunity to experience some of these things.

After a wonderful family time, full of adventures in the mountains, we returned to our home in the flatlands. The next weekend the boys and I dressed in jeans, tee-shirts and boots, with bandannas covering our heads, and makeshift eye patches resembling pirates. We scoured the fields surrounding our home in the country for the right tall, cottonwood tree.   Then we proceeded to build the world's best tree house, and this time I purchased the wood.

VIGNETTE NINE

Mentha piperita *(botanical name)* **Peppermint** *(common name): Peppermint grows to heights of three feet in clumps, although the majority of the plant hugs closely to the ground, and prefers moist, fertile, composted soil. Peppermint is a hardy perennial propagated mostly through division of clumps and seed. Gardeners need to take great care when using this plant in a garden because it will take over. The Peppermint will spread also by underground rhizomes. It grows well in full sun or minimal shade. It provides interest when mixed in gardens or contained in an herb garden or barrels, but again must be constantly pruned if the desire is to keep it contained. The jagged, pointy leaves are used in cooking, and are best when used in fresh summer tea.*

As a child, I dug up some mint that grew wild a few miles from my house with the hopes of surprising my parents with some wild, mint tea. The mint did quite well, so well in fact that it soon overtook everything in its path. I remember my father cursing the "damn stuff" for infiltrating his rose beds and trying to figure out how it had been introduced to his garden. My mother insisted on an "English garden" nestled by the porch. On the border of her small plot ran the line of mint that I had a mischievous hand secreting into the garden. The mint would, when wet, give a spicy aroma to the entire backyard.

I spent a great deal of time building my spice and herb garden boxes early in the mornings that summer, before the sun peaked from beneath the cover of eastern soil, and before my two sleepy little boys sought me out to play. I framed the boxes out of untreated railroad timbers, and imagined the savory spices that would grow within them.

On this particular morning, I had spent the majority of my time in the herb garden pulling back handfuls of spicy mint and clipping off bolting seeds on the ends of the oregano. I used a new pair of gardening shears I had found in a special order catalog. They had a plastic dipped handle and razor sharp blade. One of life's simple pleasures is having the right tools to do a job. I would hang the mint upside down in the basement to dry, and then use it as tea, both hot and cold. My mother, never a big coffee drinker, favored tea. She would serve hot tea in the winter a lot and I developed a taste for it as a child. The tea then was mostly rich, black tea with milk and lemon, not the herbal tea so popular today.

She looked to the mug of coffee that I had steaming on the porch. I wondered if she missed the tastes of food and drink. I asked her if heaven had the gourmet treats that she loved so much here in life. She never answered my questions exactly; she seemed more intent on observation and knew her purpose here during these visits.

I noticed the way the creeping mint seemed to find it's way among all of the other plantings even across the yard. I recalled a time that my mother hiked with my older brother and me along the creeks and cliffs of an area outside of Fort Collins, Colorado called Fossil Creek. We were coming down a trail leading out of the fossil formations embedded in a cliff when we were totally overwhelmed by the smell of mint. Wild mint grew in the area beneath a damp rock outcropping in the creek bed. As we began our decent to the creek bed, the loose sandstone gave way and we slid into the patch of mint. We smelled like an "Altoid" tin and soon found ourselves rolling in the mint, laughing uproariously.

I will never forget the look on my father's face when the three of us came home green-stained and covered with sandstone mud, smelling like we had been dipped in a tea of mint. I believe the jeans that I was wearing never released the minty smell even after numerous washings. My mother had a way of turning otherwise negative events into positive learning experiences. She would often laugh out loud at my zany humor and would ask me to put on silly little charades and plays to feed her humor.

Spices add to life; the tastes, and the smells all help to make otherwise bland events more tolerable and more pleasurable. People that inject a lot of personality into the daily human interactions allow life to be just that much more enjoyable. She was one of those people with her eccentricities and her viewpoint on life. Events that would bring the average human being to their knees seemed to compel her on and make her want more of the discussion, the experience, to stretch her previous conceptions and to tax her brain in a new way. It was like she wanted to experience all of the various issues of life so she in her own way could tame them. She would draw a great amount of pleasure in analyzing the daily travails of the human experience. I remember many a time when she would laugh so hard that she would end up choking or spewing her drink, and that would put us all in a tailspin. Try that at the dinner table sometime and keep a straight face.

One of the peculiar things she would do when I was a child was to encourage me to tell her friends dirty jokes, not tasteless jokes, but jokes that had a double entendre, especially Catholic jokes, and since we were Catholic, it was okay. My friends thought it was so "cool" that I could say things to my mother that would earn them a trip to the sink for a good mouthful of soap. She was advanced in age when I was growing up. Because she had waited until forty to begin her family, she was fifteen to twenty years older than most of my friends' parents. The common thought is that she would have been too old to have fun with us. By the time I was nearing my teens, she was in her fifties; the time most people have already begun the process of launching their families out into the world. Yet she was still dealing with pre-teenagers and all of the experiences this would bring.

I would go to bed nightly with the haunting tune from The Perry Mason show playing downstairs on our family room television. My mother's favorite nocturnal activities included reading deep into the night from some murder mystery or helping Perry Mason and his team to solve one of their numerous murder cases. To this day, if I catch a rerun of the old black and white Perry Mason shows, my mind reels back to the strange, comforting feeling of the nights in my childhood home as I lay in my bed under my covers lulled to sleep by the familiar, haunting melody.

As I hammered lightly on the redwood railroad ties, I noticed that she was sitting on the teak bench across the lawn. She watched the little, red foxes that had built their den on a small cliff behind our house. The pups were rolling each other down the hill from their den hole and cavorting playfully in the early morning sunlight. She spoke slowly to me. It was an early Friday morning, and she wondered what I would do that evening with my family. She wondered if I had carried on our Friday evening traditions. I had been very busy with my business and was not spending as much time with my family as usual. This seemed to concern her and she warned me about the trap of putting work first when there were so many other things of more importance.

She reminded me of the many Friday nights I had as a child. Even when I was quite young she would allow my brother and me to stay up as late as we wanted. She must have known the extra sleep on Saturday mornings would replenish us. She always said if you were tired you'd sleep, and if you were hungry, you'd eat. She herself loved the nights and late evenings and would not deprive me of them...the house so quiet at night, with the rest of the household asleep, and the world shut down to allow renewal for the next day. As a child, every Friday night for years, my mother, brother and I would make a huge batch of buttered popcorn, and select two Shasta sodas apiece. The soda choices were a wide range from root beer to red cream soda, lemon-lime, grape to cola. She would keep our soda stash replenished for our Friday "dates" with her.

Creature Features were one of my favorite childhood pastimes. Every Friday night on Creature Features, they would play two monster movies. Old black and white classics like the Vampire, Werewolf and Frankenstein movies. I have watched the television page for years hoping to see some of these old classics. The only time I have caught a glimpse is during the Halloween season. With all of the slasher movies and the movies that have desensitized the youth with the onslaught of violence, I am sure that the ratings on these classics would not satisfy the advertisers who depend on the ratings to sell their wares. It is a shame. The old black and white thrillers were charming and entertaining. Later, as a teenager, a new series called Sci-Fi Theater came on in Creature Features' place. Although I don't think she was as interested in the science fiction movies, she still sat up with me and watched them.

My wife and I started a tradition in our family called "family movie night". We popped popcorn and drank sodas on an old blanket laid out on the floor in the family room. We started with a science fiction classic about an alien eyeball from outer space. My children were so terrified by it that we decided to switch to more benign Disney movies. I remembered what it was like to sit mesmerized with my mother as we were passively and tantalizingly entertained.

VIGNETTE TEN

Syringa vulgaris *(botanical name)* **Lilac** *(common name):*
*The Lilac grows to a height of fifteen feet and can spread to
twelve feet in width. Lilacs grow in an upright fashion and if
pruned properly, can be trained into either a bush or tree.
They make for a very attractive hedge for those with the
patience to prune it meticulously. Lilacs prefers moist, fertile
composted soil and can be propagated by cuttings. They
will grow well in full sun or minimal shade, and provide
beautiful fragrance with clusters of flowers in the late spring
and early summer months. The fragrant flowers range from
white and lavender, bluish, purple and cerise. The heart
shaped leaves are glossy and pretty as a taller planting in a
perennial garden.*

*The Lilacs that grew near my bedroom window as a child,
provided shade and beauty with their numerous clusters of
lavender flowers. They had a prominent and significant
position in the garden. I always knew that they had a
special place in my mother's heart. I would often notice that
she would spend time near them when she needed to
meditate and draw strength from their position of solitude in
the garden. Every year she would bring in numerous
bouquets of their fragrant flowers, and place them around
the house perfuming our entire home. I remember she
seemed both happy and sad during the weeks when they
bloomed.*

I found that the perfect place to put the lilac bushes was off of the main patio in my backyard. The lilacs provided beautiful foliage all summer but, particularly in the early spring, they would grace my yard with the fragrance of my childhood. It is interesting to me, as I now realize, that I had placed the lilacs in my backyard in about the same position as my mother and father had in their backyard when I was still a child. Although not intentional, or even noticed at the time on my part, I feel sure now that it was some small piece of a master gardener's plan. They were truly in the most optimal place in the yard and sheltered over fifty plantings of various colored pansies, columbines and other creeping beauties. I had noted a very large lilac in a neighborhood that had been pruned to "tree" and decided I would begin the process of pruning one of mine to take on the shape of a tree rather than that of a bush. The issue with lilacs is that they colonize and in order to truly "tree", they must be diligently pruned to shape. The result was a majestic tree that looked over the backyard and provided blooms at the height that they could be enjoyed from the elevated back deck.

As I labored about with my pruners, visualizing the gardens shown in various magazines that seemed to stretch for miles, and wondering why I hadn't bought a smaller house with a larger yard, I noticed her again in the garden. She paused across the lawn near the vegetables, and was gazing at the tomatoes. She seemed to long to touch the Roma tomatoes hanging over the whiskey barrel in the corner of the yard. They were her favorites in life. She used them in her sauces and sliced thin in salads. She could do wonders with a tomato, cucumber, onions, basil leaves and other vinegary sauces that I have never been able to replicate in my own kitchen. I have the raw ingredients and the desire to once again taste her recipes, but I lack the deep, creative comprehension of the harmony and the blending that was her second nature. I wish now that I had spent more hours in the kitchen with her, learning her craft. How much we miss of those around us that offer so much. I wish I hadn't waited so long. There is no way to predict what time is left for our relationships. What is certain is that if we touch each other with as much love as possible now, we will not live on with regret.

Until I became an avid gardening enthusiast and an aspiring chef, I had never understood the great symbiosis between my parents. My father's hours toiling in the vegetable garden provided her with the ingredients for her craft in the kitchen. She had been such a wonderful cook, and of course as a child, I was quite unappreciative of her talents. My friends would usually come from dinner describing the usual American dinner fare -- hamburgers, hot dogs, macaroni and cheese -- which I would envy. I would plead to spend the night with them the next weekend, so I could experience the normal "good" dinners they took for granted. Now I long to once again taste from her kitchen one of her creations.

Our common dinner was something lifted right out of a Julia Child's program. My mother would snip herbs from the garden to enhance the flavors of her delectable dishes. Variety was the norm. Tens of hundreds of cookbooks were stacked downstairs near her "sewing room". During the hours that she would spend creating, numerous others lay dog-eared and splattered by sauces and "spoon tastes" in the kitchen as she would create her "masterpieces". As an adult, I find it very interesting that she was so consumed with cooking and the fineries of the gourmet kitchen, yet she never tipped the scale over ninety pounds.

As I returned to pruning the lilacs in my yard, she communicated her deep love for my father. She indicated that he was lonely and needed me to draw close and assist him in his ongoing loss of her. I sensed that she might have also been trying to reach him, probably in his garden, which he still spends many hours toiling in. She asked me to be the one to be with him, to assure him of life ongoing, to assure him of the eternal with belief he might someday join her again.

One of the true gifts my parents gave me as a child has manifested itself in a great marriage in my own life. I have a marriage as strong as any I know of because we share our hearts. From my part, I am able to do so largely because of the observations as a child of a marriage that worked...a union of compromises, a willingness to give when it hurt, a marriage viewed without exit doors. As a young adult my mother and father shared candidly how often they had come to an impasse on issues, but through hours of communication, always worked their issues out. My consistent observation was of a couple in love with each other and dedicated to the success of their relationship. They had a deepness lacking so much in many marriages today. To make sure this doesn't sound too much like Ward and June Cleaver, they had their problems, too. Many problems, as a matter of fact. As an adult I reflect on, and wonder, how two people with so many differences weathered a marriage for so many years; yet their similarities were many. They shared a deep love for the same things in life; of music, food, travel, art and those things that bring true depth in the spirit. As a child, it was not uncommon to see my mother pat my father's rump or whisper something in his ear, an obvious secret of love. Activities my brother and I would shun off as "gross". Watching your parents love one another gives you a true deep security as a child.

I recollect a time when I was quite young. My mother and father brought home the large green lilac bushes and spoke as though they were of great significance to the house. It meant very little to me as they deliberated for hours the proper place for them. I had noted that my mother and my father looked very sad. She was in a mood unusual to her house, a mood of melancholy. They also brought a charred, red brick into the house and placed it prominently on a shelf near the mantle of the fireplace. It was done in such a sorrowful, ceremonious way, that it was etched in my mind as relevant. It seemed odd to me at the time that an otherwise lovely set of thick oak shelves would be a resting place for an old, charred brick, but it was not something my brother or I felt comfortable asking about at the time.

I spent many winter evenings at the fireplace. It was an old-fashioned fireplace twice as deep and twice as wide as you find in the common tract homes of today. The mantle was a large slab of oak, and the red bricks were set off by a large piece of thick, crimson flagstone. I would sit on cold winter nights reading a book or petting my old dog as the fire crackled behind me, warming my back; a comforting feeling on a cold, snowy, wintry night. The old brick was significant, though I would not fully understand it's gravity until I was old enough, (as a teenager), to hear the story recounted at dinner one night.

My parents had both been in academia and had started their early careers at the University. They had offices in an old building endeared to all as the "Old Main". Their budding careers and their blossoming romance took place within the red brick walls of the classically styled building. In the early sixties during one of the many student protests, Old Main was burned to the ground. My parents grieved the building as they would have an old friend. To bring a part of it home, they went and salvaged a brick from the charred remains and dug out three small lilacs that had grown near and survived the heat of the inferno which had stolen an important part of their history and their early love for one another.

The fragrance would waft through the early summer evening air, and I could smell the strong floral perfume even half a mile away. I knew summer was coming soon when my room smelled of lilac. The lilacs now have crept higher than the house of my childhood and stand in prominence and importance. The current tenants of the home have no way of understanding what the lilacs that dignify their house stand for; a symbol of a love that perhaps started under a lilac tree in the years of yesterday...when life was simpler and the Cadillacs still had wings.

VIGNETTE ELEVEN

Geranium himaleyense *(botanical name)* **Blue Cranesbill** *(common name): The Blue Cranesbill grows to one foot in a mounded, spreading habit. It will grow nicely in well-drained soil in sun or partial shade. Blue Cranesbill provides color in spring and early summer. Its beautiful lilac-blue flowers and light-green serrated foliage can be added to rock gardens and borders.*

To the south of my childhood bedroom window, my father had placed a staggered red stone walking path which encircled three quarters of the house. Between the flagstones were various plantings. The most common of them on the outside of the staggered path was the Blue Cranesbill. The vibrant color was apparent from all parts of the backyard. I remember once near dusk, when I was supposed to be going to sleep, I observed from my bedroom window my parents dancing slowly and closely to a classical song by Chopin or Brahms. Their dance started on the back patio and went across the flagstones. She bent over and plucked a flower from one of the Blue Cranesbills and placed it in her mouth in the fashion of a Spanish dancer. They laughed and held each other tightly and then disappeared around the house.

The first few times she visited me, even though it was comforting, it was still unsettling. When you say good-bye one final time, it is the generally accepted belief that communication with a loved one now gone, is only in the imagination and in prayers. The fact that you generally remember and converse with a loved one in your own mind is a built-in comforter. The visits in my garden have been genuine and meaningful. When it started, except for the first time on the night of her "death", it was an effort to communicate because of the usual doubt and conditioning we mere mortals, with our limited understanding of the enormity surrounding us, possess. Our tendency is to not trust the possibility of the unknown. It was my intention, at first, to learn as much as possible from these encounters. Now it is more like being wrapped in a warm blanket in the frigid winter months.

There was a morning in mid-July, one of those uncommon times when the sense of well being within me was overwhelming. The sky had opened up around midnight the previous evening and showered the earth intensely, leaving a deep, earthy, woody smell and a dampness that penetrates skin and bone. My first inclination was to lie in bed and relax and listen to the soft breeze and the serenade of the birds in the fluttering aspens below my bedroom window. I thought better of the idea and went to the kitchen, tiptoeing to avoid awakening the rest of the house. Ten minutes later, I sat on the front porch and sipped a deep brew of French Roast coffee and settled back to read the Sunday morning installment of the news. Within a few moments I had tired of reading about the travails and sorrows that my fellow humans had caused each other in the preceding days. I found myself gazing into the deep lilac of a blue cranesbill. Wandering to the front flower bed, and sipping slowly on the gratifying coffee in the mug, I stepped across some damp, cedar wood chips surrounding a large, moss rock and aspen planting to inspect some geraniums I had potted over the last winter for a break from the barren winter months.

As incense permeates a room when lit, a strong scented combination of lemon, cedar and the loamy smell of earth filled the front yard and carried me back to a rainy summer day in my youth. I remember running barefoot across very hot asphalt as the sky darkened and threatened to break loose a deluge of water. I was playing a childhood game with some of the neighbor children, enjoying a hot summer day. When the sky finally opened up, drops of rain as large as fifty-cent pieces cascaded onto the asphalt. I swear you could hear a sizzling noise, and the smell of the hot rain welled up and suddenly my whole world became a sauna. Then shortly it was like a steam room, and then as the rain cooled off the earth, the gutters filled and became a cool watery delight. We jumped off the curbs and took delight in the splashing of water. The streets had become a large amusement park.

As the rain subsided, one of the older boys introduced us younger boys to the mystery of the cigarette. They were lemon flavored and burned deeply in my lungs, as the older boy had, in a menacing way, convinced us to breath it in as deeply as possible. When I returned to the house I must have reeked of cigarette smoke. Upon my arrival home, my mother smelled the smoke on my clothes and then lit a whole pack of cigarettes, one after another and "let" me smoke them on the back porch as she watched me get sicker and sicker. I was cured. I would not desire the musty smoke in my lungs again. She had calculated the outcome before it happened.

As I awakened from my trance, I realized the lemon scented geraniums planted at the base of one of the aspens in my front yard, had brought on the memory as I dazed off into another morning in summer. As I brought myself back from my childhood once again, she stood near me observing me curiously. This time my dog saw her too. The hair bristled up on the mutt's back and she produced a low growl. I stroked her back and convinced her that the visitor was a welcome one indeed.

She seemed to be telling me again something in a very gentle way, something about my father. She came this time to remind me that it wasn't merely she who had sought me out as an infant, but my father also. He and I never really shared the close bond she and I had. He was generally a melancholy person and had a hard time getting out of the intellectual, freeing himself to simply play. He spent countless hours in his garden when I was a child, and it was there I would share time with him. It was there our paths crossed as best they could between two people so different. Although we were generally cut from a different cloth, and his ways most often were, and are, a mystery to me, as mine are to him, he had a distinct gentleness about him. His generally gentle way with his children allowed me to be a boy with emotions, instead of a "macho" man who showed his worth through his athletic prowess and toughness only, as so many of my friends were forced to do.

When I would be in some deep childhood despair, it was not uncommon for my father to take me into his lap and "wy wy" me to sleep, a deep balm to my soul. "Wy wy" was what he would sing over and over in my ear, which had the affect of gently lulling me to sleep and allowing a new perspective on the current tragedy by the separation of sweet slumber. He "wy wy'd" me more times than I can count. I have "wy wy'd" my own boys over the years. It was a magical time between us, and has allowed me to present my father's sweet legacy to his grandchildren.

She was clear in her communication and seemed to be anxious to impress upon me that my father needed me to be close. To let him know I cared, she wanted me to share the experience of our visits with him. The idea of sharing these moments with him did not appeal to me. He, an avowed agnostic, would never find credence or relevance in these tales of time with his beloved and now departed wife. They were married nearly thirty years and he was still intensely bonded with her. He took losing her very badly, and was still not able to come to terms with it.

It is this she had come to show me; that I needed to allow my father a relationship with me also, although it would be quite different from the one I had shared with her. It, too, could be one of closeness and meet the mutual needs we had for one another; a father and a son as adults, equals yet still very different, the way they had been. I had already tried many times to make a connection with him. It was strained and forced and I think we both felt it. It is a peculiar situation when two people desire a closeness, but cannot find their way to it. Some relationships are meant to be and others are meant to be tried again and again.

I went to him and shared the experience of my first meeting with my mother. His reaction was instant and deep. He cried, and I could tell he was struggling all at once with the whole concept of life hereafter; of God, eternity, and the promise of heaven. It was the first time in my life that I felt I had "wy wy'd" my own father.

"...a love that perhaps started under a lilac tree in the years of yesterday...when life was simpler and the Cadillacs still had wings."

VIGNETTE TWELVE

Picea pungens 'Glauca' *(botanical name)* **Blue Spruce** *(common name): The Blue Spruce is native to Colorado and will grow to over one hundred feet. The beautiful tree prefers moist, fertile, composted soil in full sun and will tolerate hostile weather conditions, which makes it a wonderful tree to plant in the yards of the gardener who wants a low maintenance tree which will, in the years to come, provide a lot of shade. The Blue Spruce is generally propagated by transplanting, most commonly as a burlaped or a balled tree, but for the very patient can be cultured by bare-root seedlings. They provide a pretty conical shaped tree with blue needles which add an unusual color to the landscape.*

When my father received his doctorate, my mother had a Blue Spruce planted off of the back patio to symbolize the accomplishment. The tree was slow growing and stood out for years as a great symbol of my father's dedication and hard work. I have noticed when I have returned to the backyard of my youth, that one of the subsequent owners has removed the Blue Spruce, a true shame. Had they known the symbolism of the tree, they might have let it tower in its rightful place.

I was startled by the sound of the geese honking in formation overhead. They were once again headed south for the winter. They seemed to be mocking me and my heavy earthbound arms. With the wind lifting their downy bodies across the pale blue sky and their carefree and wonderful view of all of the gardens stretching from here to the south, I envied them and wondered where this flock would land for these upcoming winter months.

The slight chill cast over the earth around me threatened to end the growth around the yard for another season of dormancy. The lilacs and pear trees were showing hints of reds and yellows in their leaves, and some hyacinth bulbs were forcing grass-like growth underneath the trees. The second fall planting of peas was becoming just a trickle, scarcely enough to harvest. The tomatoes made their last effort, and the spinach ready to finish off made me long for another three months of the vegetable garden. The weather forecast was for our first snow, (not a big deal). In Colorado you often experience a snow one day and then sunny, seventy-degree weather the next day, in both autumn and spring.

Autumn is always a time of reflection for me; the bittersweet emotions of winding down another garden and retreating inside for the "hibernation" period. The longing to feel earth on my hands is barely quieted by my tinkering with an "inside garden". Each fall, my last traditional effort at salvaging the gardening urge is to plant at least a clump of tulips, daffodils, hyacinths or crocus somewhere in the yard where my garden diary indicates "lacked for color or interest" in the earliest of spring months. The display from the planting of the bulbs, is something I look forward to throughout the cold, hard winter months, and provides the last true dirt to cover my hands for the season.

The grow lamps and the window boxes cannot replicate the feel of the earth in the garden. It is a pleasure to taste of fresh basil during the snowy months and of the other herbs in the window box of the sink in the kitchen that we harvest for hot teas to sip while curling up with a good book by the fire. It is the tastes and textures of the fresh garden tomatoes and the crispness of peas, onions and snap beans that I long for during the winter. The geraniums, with their powerful colors and distinctive scents in the windows, gently remind me of the upcoming spring and the promises that the soil holds for another season of gardening joy.

Soon the snap of frost would end the season and the activities would turn to costumes for trick-or-treating, turkey dinners and family gatherings. Then Christmas would dominate at least a month with its traditional preparations, shopping and dinner parties. Life is full of its own seasons. If the winter didn't come and bring to closure some of the seasonal gardens, we would too soon take for granted the warm months spent puttering about in the flower and vegetable gardens. In the same way life tends to run its course through a series of seasons and events that lead to a new growth. The "winters" of life allow us to draw inward, to reflect and to slow down, to allow ourselves the season to catch up and revitalize.

Each season holds it's own charm, and it is vital that we learn to love them all. In the same way, we must learn to fully enjoy each season in our lives before they, too, will end and be replaced by another. When the gardens are bursting forth with all of the splendor and color, there is not much opportunity to reflect and study the single beauties which are coming forth. In the winter, the few forcing bulbs, herbs and geraniums are singled out for their bounty and beauty in a very different way than the masses outside.

I had been pruning the undergrowth of my three new "babies"...beautiful blue spruces. I was wiping alcohol across the blades of the pruning shears. It is important to do so in case one of the trees holds a communicable disease that should not be spread to the other trees in the yard. It is fascinating to watch what the blue spruce does within a month of a major pruning. Bright, almost translucent-blue buds of new growth pop out all over the top and the outside branches. The conical tree always makes me think of Christmas. The smell of pine floats through the house when the newly cut tree is brought into the room near the fireplace. The trees in my adult home are covered with the old and the new ornaments, hand-picked carefully by my wife and me, as well as those that held specific meaning to my parents.

Many were my mother's favorites, and the long strand of pearl-colored beads adorn the tree near the top every year. It was the first ornament that my parents used. A small glass bird perches on a bow and a small silver Swiss bell hangs near the bottom of the tree. The little bell was purchased by me in a small German town in Kansas when I was quite young. It was the first present that I ever purchased with money I had earned by myself, and I bought it as a Christmas gift for my parents.

Ave Maria is the song that completely captures the essence of Christmas for me; both the melody and the meaning. I find the music to be a moving piece in the same way that Beethoven's *Moonlight Sonata* can evoke a deep, ethereal emotion. Christmas is many people's favorite time of the year. It is also a difficult time of year for many. It is difficult for me because it is so far from the time my hands will once again be warmed by the rich soil in the garden. The plants and even grow lights and seed starts do not replicate the feeling of toiling in the gardens.

But Christmas holds its mysteries and delights in it's own way. Some of my fondest childhood memories are of events that took place during the Christmas season. My mother would make it special. One tradition that she had brought from the old country was a German custom of waiting until it was Christmas eve to decorate the tree. She was one for tradition, and the tradition that annoyed my brother and me to no end, was her insistence on having a nut dish which made us wait for Christmas. The nut dish was a throwback from her childhood when times were simple and gifts would be contained in the simple dish. It had evolved to being just that in our family, a dish full of nuts, fruit and Christmas candies. She would place everyone's dish in its respective place and read from *The Night Before Christmas*, illustrated by Grandma Moses. After what seemed like hours, we finally got to open the presents. Interestingly, I have made my own children go through a similar tradition. We said as children that we would never do that to our children. I guess the anticipation building is part of the magic. We do get the tree a month before Christmas, -- my way of setting our own tradition.

The geese had been right. Their flight southward was instinctive. It is wondrous how the simple creatures have an internal mechanism allowing them to understand their own needs for preservation. The weathermen had predicted that we would get a light snow, from a dusting to possibly two inches. That night in mid-September, when the trees usually begin their beautiful transformation and ready themselves for a winter sleep by shunning their growth and going inward and dormant, an unexpected snow storm hit Colorado. An arctic front, down from Canada, came and wiped the landscape away the way a large grizzly wipes away the life of its prey with one swipe. The snow was heavy and wet and took a dramatic toll on the trees everywhere. I looked out at the snow covered landscape and realized it had taken trees, tomatoes, cucumbers, flowers, thousands of sprinkling systems and all of my hundreds of plants, which lay beneath a foot of early, wet, autumn snow. Trees were literally split in half. I drove around the city remorseful at the loss. So many trees devastated, so much torn apart by the senseless event. That night, the temperature dropped forty degrees within an eight hour period. The devastation this did to my spirit and my beautifully tended garden, was the same way death had come and taken my mother's life.

The next spring, many of the trees that had been damaged by the storm early in September, came back with a renewed vigor. The limbs which had broken off in the brutal snow seemed to push their strength back into the trees. The foliage showed new life and beauty that hadn't been there before. The bulbs broke through the warming soil and made the departing winter a memory. Everything came back with a renewed strength and resolve, and seemed even better than it had been before.

This was God's message to me through her visits. Life is a pattern of beginnings, renewal and loss. Her life had been an imprint on this earth, one that no other human had or would ever have. Her unique imprint on this earth was similar to a single snowflake, beautiful and unique from all of the others and destined to fall in a specific place for it's impact. She reminded me with the visits that we must all leave an imprint of some kind, an emblem of importance...that the relevance of God's people is significant and eternal...the way that we are toward each other on this earth will affect the generations down the line. The main thing to internalize for me, is that we all come packaged with our good and our bad constitution. The key in our relationships is to accept and to love without strings. The Agape-style of love that we can show each other is one that liberates relationships beyond our limited expectations of one another and simply celebrates the human touch that we can enjoy.

A few springs later, Mrs. Stroh left the earthbound suit she had worn for so many years. As she would have wanted, she slipped away comfortably in her porch rocker, probably looking out on the new life springing forth with its colors. I wonder who will be graced with garden visits from her?

*"She continued on the issue
of God's desire for His human race
to learn to love for the sake of love itself."*

EPILOGUE

A garden at night is a most beautiful thing. It is a wondrous thing to linger in a garden under the cover of stars, the perspective one can gain by listening only to a cricket chorus is amazing. The fragrance of the blooms and the grapey, "citrus" smells from the luscious petals and the wet mulch combine to alert the senses to the balance of nature. The moon was full and the familiar presence was once again with me in the garden. It had been several years since her last visit, and I had begun to think God's gift of her visits to my garden were to be confined to a few seasons of my gardens and my life. A slight breeze blew over my naked torso as I stood on the back porch looking at the silvery light blanketing the flowers. The textures of the near black and white landscape held an eerie mystique. As I began to descend the stairs from the back redwood deck to the gardens below, I realized that she was sitting on the teak bench at the back of the vegetable garden. Nights were cooling off and the late summer plantings of peas and spinach were emerging in a splendid dance with the stars. The pods formed even as the small plants were breaking through the surface of the earth. The destination of all that is green is to instinctively reinvent itself, which in turn provides the bounty of the harvest for us.

That night would be her last visit. It was that night that she left me to stand on my own. She never explained the reasons for her visits and I remember at the time wanting to know more about their purposes. I have learned since that there were many reasons I was gifted with the visits. Many seasons and summers have now passed and she has not returned. I long to reach out for her, to say hello once again, but I was gifted in a way few of God's creatures are, and I will never forget her in life or death and the hereafter, for she did, in fact, help make me the man that I have become; a man who is genuinely tender with children as she was with me, loving with my wife as she was with my father, and a friend who can be relied upon and trusted as she was. I now say a final good-bye to her and thank her for all of the wonderful life she brought to mine. For those who do not believe in the hereafter, there is the resolution that we do live on eternally. If not through the traditional beliefs of Heaven and Hell, it is a fact that the spark or the essence of the person lives on in the descendants and friends left behind. The special touch and "fingerprint" which we leave on each other will influence in some way eternally. Make sure that the mark we leave is a legacy that we would desire to be our lasting impression.

She continues to "visit" me periodically in the memories of my wonderful childhood that she had so much of a hand in providing me with. In many senses, she is with me continuously through the indelible imprint which she made on my personality and love for life. I now have the balance of retrospection, to understand that she was lovely, yet flawed like a rose. No single flower is perfect in it's own right, but as a member of the respective whole it can contribute to the beauty of the gardens that we walk through.

I now can say, "Good-bye mother, I will miss your company forever. You were one of the most beautiful roses whom God has put in this man's earthly gardens."

I would advise you to reflect on the people around you who are special to you, to thank them, and to forgive them for anything that is left unsettled. For those who have left you, but will reside in your memory as long as you live in God's garden, I would counsel you to open up to the teachings from them that will take place if you yield yourself to them. Your own garden visits can take place if it is the will of your Creator and if it is your will to learn. In order to fully absorb the wonders that surround us, we must take the necessary time to ponder, to share, to love each other and ourselves. Why do you think the old saying holds that you have to take time to stop and smell the roses?

THE END...or just the beginning?

About the Author

Justin Matott wrote *My Garden Visits* as a tribute to the memory of his mother. Through much encouragement to publish this book by friends and family, he has realized the dream of being a published author. Mr. Matott lives in Colorado and is currently working on his third novel and a children's book series.

About the Illustrator

Victoria Kwasinski holds a Bachelor of Fine Arts degree in Illustration and has received numerous awards for her work. The watercolor illustrations were done without the aid of "pre-drawn" lines to add to the freshness and spontaneity of each image. Ms. Kwasinski works from her studio in Littleton, Colorado.

To order additional copies of *My Garden Visits*, or for further information about the work of Mr. Matott or Ms. Kwasinski, please contact :

CLOVE PUBLICATIONS
PO Box 261183
Littleton, Colorado 80163-1183